Mud City

A FLAMINGO STORY

Brenda Z. Guiberson

HENRY HOLT AND COMPANY · NEW YORK

A mother flamingo sits on a muddy nest in the Bahamas and reaches out to scoop up a beakful of ooze. *Splop!* She slaps the mud onto the side of the twelve-inch-high mound. The shallow lake is crowded with flamingos. A few stand on a toothpick leg and doze. Others dip their heads upside down into the salty water to eat. But most sit on a mud nest to shade an egg from the blistering sun.

The mother gets up to stretch. The father rolls the egg over with his beak and shakes mud off his feet before taking a turn on the nest. It is so hot the air shimmers. The lake water evaporates quickly, leaving salt crystals behind.

The mud city is twice as salty as the sea, and not much can live there. The flamingos cry super-salty teardrops to get rid of the extra salt.

The mangrove trees have adapted too. Salt seeps out through their leaves. *Plop!* When a leaf drops off, the salt is gone. The underwater leaves are then attacked by bacteria and fungi. Soon they will rot into food for the tiny brine shrimp and mollusks that the flamingos eat.

The mother flamingo leaves the crowded mud city and flies across the tropical island, looking for somewhere else to eat. She passes Bahama parrots gorging on fruit.

She swoops over vast acres where workers pump ocean water into shallow ponds and wait for the sun and wind to dry out the salt crystals. Some are piled into glittery mountains. Other crystals are loaded into a ship. Eventually they will be sprinkled on food and icy roads. The flamingo finally finds a pink pond where she can rest and eat.

As dark clouds blow toward the island, the mother flamingo returns to the mud city. Soon the rain falls in sheets and the lake churns and spits. Big waves surge into the lowest area and flood the nests.

Flapflapflap! Wings pump and pink legs splash in frantic circles. The water swirls off with many of the eggs. Some are broken by stamping flamingo feet. Much of the nesting area is a disaster.

The mother and father made their nest on high ground near the mangrove trees, whose tangled roots trap mud and build up the land. The birds' egg is safe, and they continue to shade it from the sun. They take baths in the new rain puddles and drink the fresh water. Herons, egrets, and spoonbills join them on the edges of the refreshed lake.

Peck, peck, peck! After four weeks a fluffy white chick hatches. He struggles up on wobbly pink legs and huge webbed feet. *Kah, kah!* He flaps his tiny wings.

Both parents have glands in their throats that make a red liquid full of fat and protein. They take turns dribbling this flamingo "milk" into the chick's small, straight beak.

For the next three days the parents sit on the nest to protect the chick. The rain puddles dry up as new chicks hatch across the muddy nursery.

On the fourth day the baby takes his first slide down the side of the nest. *Splosh!* When he lands in the water he already knows how to swim. The warm trade winds blow him across the lake with a crèche, or group of young birds.

The parents fly out to other salty lakes, called salinas, for more food. Sometimes they migrate hundreds of miles during the night before returning to feed the chick.

At five weeks the chick has new gray feathers and strong black legs. His beak is now long and curved, and he tries to eat like the adults. *Tramp, tramp, stamp!* He dances in a circle to stir up food from the muddy bottom. With his head upside down he uses his tongue to pump water and strain out brine shrimp.

The warm shrimp soup is full of carotenoids, the same chemicals that make carrots orange. The carotenoids add color to the water and even to the flamingos. The chick will soon grow a few pink feathers of his own.

It hasn't rained for several weeks, and now the lake is three times as salty as the sea. Food is scarce, and the adult birds have left for good. The little flamingo must learn to fly or he will starve.

Splish, splash, splash! He
runs through the water.

Fwop fwop fwop. Finally
he lifts into the air.

Flying is tricky, but landing is hard too. One foot down, now two feet. *Sploosh!* The chick ends his first flight upside down and soggy.

Soon the young flamingo can fly longer distances. He swoops around a pelican and swerves over cactuses and clattering crabs. He tires quickly and splashes into a turquoise lagoon.

The fresh seawater is not as salty as the mud city. It is an ocean nursery filled with razzle-dazzle fish, waving tentacles, and even baby sharks. The flamingo watches them all.

Crunch, crunch! A parrotfish nibbles on the coral. As it crunches it turns the coral into new sand. The little flamingo stamps in the sand for food. *Swoosh!* A spotted eagle ray shoots up from its hiding place and glides away. The flamingo steps back on a sea hare. *Squirt!* The squishy creature shoots out a cloud of purple ink.

The tired flamingo returns to the mud city with the other young birds. The lake continues to dry up, and circles can be seen in the cracked mud where the birds danced.

It is a good thing the flamingo is three months old and has the feathers needed for long flight. There is little left in the salina except powdery mud, mosquitoes, and clumps of dazzling salt.

The eggs of the brine shrimp are now hard cysts. As cysts they can survive for days, months, even years without water. When it rains again they will bloom into a new salty soup for the flamingos.

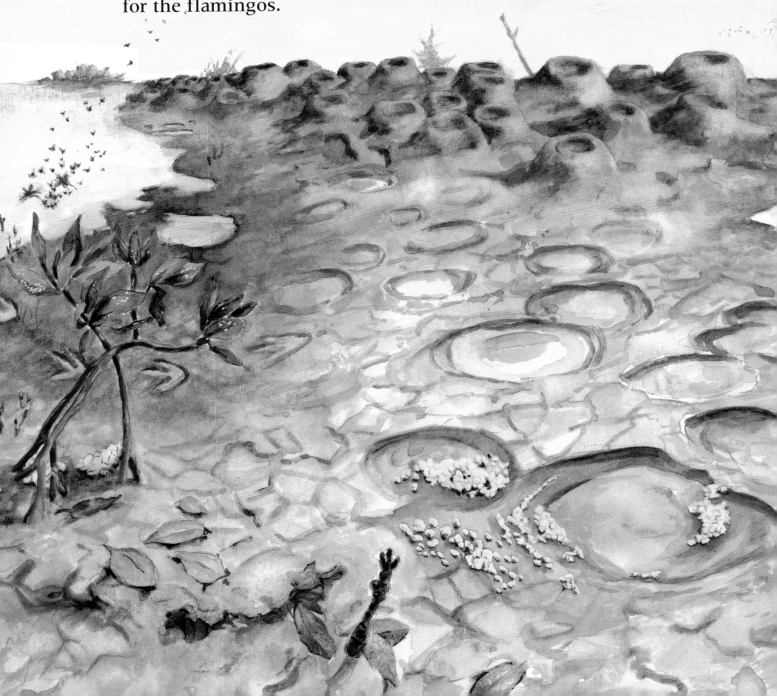

Over the next three years the bird grows tall and more colorful. Like all flamingos he is skittish and shy. He joins flocks of other flamingos in quiet lagoons and super-salty salinas.

In the flamingo's fourth year the spring is very dry. When he joins a nesting group the water is extremely low. Wild pigs are able to trot across the dried mud and threaten the flock. The pigs smell a feast of eggs and chicks. *Snort!*

First one, then many pink necks stretch out toward the strange noise. *Snort! Snort!* The pigs are too close. The frantic birds flap away in a great pink cloud. The nests are destroyed and must be abandoned.

After five years the flamingo is grown up and restless. In March, just when his feathers are brightest and his beak is shiny, he joins a gathering flock looking for mates. *Cak! Cak!* He starts the courtship dance with a swing of his head. Other large males follow while the smaller females strut by.

Splishsplash, cak, grouk! It is a noisy water ballet with heads swinging, beaks waving, and wings snapping in a wild salute.

ZZOOM! A pilot guides his plane overhead to watch. The shy flamingos stop dancing. *Honkhonkhonk!* They take off.

The birds return to the salina rimmed by mangroves. The airspace here is reserved for flamingos. Airplanes are not allowed.

At sunrise the flock begins the courtship dance again. *Honk, snap, flap, splash.* This time the flamingo finds a mate. Like the other paired birds they scoop up clumps of mud to build a nest.

The lake is so quiet, so salty, and so hot. Few would like to live there, but it is just the right spot for the flamingos' mud city.

For the Nixon family wardens
and the people of Inagua, Bahamas,
who share their island with thousands of flamingos.
And for Marjy Fiddler, fellow traveler.

Many thanks to Laura Godwin, Reka Simonsen,
and the others at Holt who helped with this book.

Henry Holt and Company, LLC, *Publishers since 1866*
115 West 18th Street, New York, New York 10011
www.henryholt.com

Library of Congress Cataloging-in-Publication Data
Guiberson, Brenda Z.
Mud city: a flamingo story / Brenda Z. Guiberson.—1st ed.
ISBN-13: 978-0-8050-7177-1
ISBN-10: 0-8050-7177-6
1. Flamingos—Life cycles—Juvenile literature. I. Title.
QL696.C56G85 2005   598.3'5—dc22   2004009199
First Edition—2005 / Designed by Donna Mark
The artist used watercolor and gouache to create the illustrations for the book.
Printed in the United States of America on acid-free paper. ∞
1 3 5 7 9 10 8 6 4 2